Is It A Hoax

Or Is It Cheeto And His Swamp Creatures?"

An illustrated reaction on today's news.

by Janet E. Levy

Commander in Cheat
speaking nonsense

Trump's Vocabulary is a joke, I have worked with six-year-old children whose vocabulary was far more advanced than this crazed orange stain. Some "bizarre words" to name a few:

"Covfefe"

"Hamberders"

"The Cyber"

"Nambia"

"Big-League"

"My military, my generals"

"Two Corinthians"

"Bad Hombres"

"Herd mentality"

"Dumpy Frumpy, Individual One..."

The Orange "HOAX"

in Our People's House

The First Einstein Visa
First Lady "FAKE"

Ivanka, the Manipulator

Newsweek SUBSCRIBE ›

POLITICS

Twitter Mocks Ivanka Trump For Being Shunned by World Leaders at G-20: 'Bring Your Stupid Daughter to Work Day'

BY CHRISTINA ZHAO ON 6/30/19 AT 7:32 PM EDT

Ivanka
always on the News

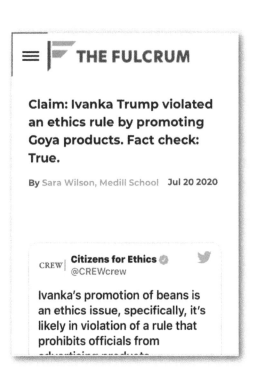

≡ ⯌ THE FULCRUM

Claim: Ivanka Trump violated an ethics rule by promoting Goya products. Fact check: True.

By Sara Wilson, Medill School   Jul 20 2020

CREW | **Citizens for Ethics** ✓
@CREWcrew

Ivanka's promotion of beans is an ethics issue, specifically, it's likely in violation of a rule that prohibits officials from

The New Norm

THE NEW NORM

These last 4 years have been surreal at best. Everything we have worked towards has been taken down by an incompetent, imbecile, narcissistic poor excuse for a human being, who calls himself the "US President".

The year 2020 will never be forgotten!

I hereby dedicate this little Silly Book to all my friends, to my son Alec P. Levy-O'Brien, Journalism student at the University of Colorado at Boulder who has been very supportive and to my sister Nora Ward who has encouraged me to move forward with my "renditions" of this era. I would also like to give Leo Baquero, the talented Designer who helped me with the layout and design of the book, responsible for giving life to my illustrations and thoughts, a big "shout out". Thank You!!!

May a Few Laughs be Enjoyed by All
with this book.

Janet E. Levy
2020

The "new Norm"

Shelter In Place (SIP)

Traveling these days? Do not forget
COVID-19 is your travel companion.

7·01·2020

The "art of how not wearing a mask",

it is not manly says the trump.

A Swampy bunch of deplorables in our administration

Who can ever forget the players in the Trump administration:

"Moscow Mitch", "Leningrad Lindsey", Gym Jordan, Matt Gaetz, William Barr, and the rest of the "Swamp Deplorables"?

Here you have a list of Trump's close associates who have faced charges:

Steve Bannon, Roger Stone, Michael Flynn, Paul Manafort, Rick Gates, Michael Cohen, George Papadopoulos.

Is the "swamp" drained yet?

Gym Jordan, is your suit jacket?

The Screamer in our House.

The Infamous Barff,
who is he trying to kid...?

Kelly Anne, Trump's sidekick...
Gone!

Roasting in an Open Fire, Baby Trump

#MoscowMitch and #BanBarf

Betzy DeWitch

Teddy the Boot Licker

(with horns)

Stone is the name

for the fancy old Gent.

GOYA Beans anyone?

Disbar The Barr

Hey "trumpfuehrer",
how does it feel being behind bars?

As seen in the wild...

TRUMPiES BABiES

Complete Failure
Pretend President

Time to have someone show you where *the door* is.

You are one *pathetic* poor excuse of a man.

YOUR IMMEDIATE RESIGNATION IS HEREBY ACCEPTED BY: "**AMERICA THE GREAT**".

- We need a Leader and this you are far from it.

- We need someone with a Soul, and this you lack.

- We need someone who is not all about "himself and this you are.

- We need someone who can Speak, Read and Write fluently and this you are not.

We don't need a *Liar* and *Thief* in our White House and this you are.

We don't need someone who is vindictive and this you are.

We don't need someone who calls himself a *"stable genius"* ...because this is Mr. Ed and not you.

#RESIGNNOW #RESIGNNOW
#TAKEYOURDEPLORALBLESWITHYOU

LADY LIBERTY
IS SO CONFUSED!

20-20 Vision

The Year 2020 affected us all one way or another.

We, **The United States of America**,
set the *World Record* during the *Pandemic*
and we are still in the thick of it.

As of *September 21, 2020* we surpassed
200,000 people dead,
with more than **6,850,000** confirmed cases ...(*and counting*)
That is **more people dead** than all US casualties in
the *Korean, Vietnam, Gulf, Afghanistan* and *Iraq* invasion wars
combined.

...And the Apprentice gives himself an **A+**
for his handling the pandemic
while blaming *China* and the *World Health Organization*
for all those deaths at
the United Nations 75th annual assembly.

Life is an adventure
when living in a PANDEMIC

Toilet paper shortage was a "result of panic buying" according to Dr. Ronald Gonzalez, an assistant Professor in the Department of Forest Biomaterials. Toilet paper became a coveted item and hoarders a nuisance, and the rest buying in Panic mode. Hand sanitizer another "coveted item", to this day there is still a shortage. I made my personal brand and gifted it to friends and family. For Health Care Workers the entire supply of PPE (Personal Protective Equipment) became a luxury and many of these folks were pleading friends and relatives to help them find these items. Face Masks, oh yes!, Face Masks which are a "controversial" item still, most of us wear them when in Public and then there are those who "complain" and refuse to wear them regardless of how much it has been proven that they help with the spread of the Virus.

No matter where we look at this Pandemic it will leave scars all over the world but particularly here in the USA because of the lack of "leadership" and how the man living in our People's House refuses to take responsibility and do something positive that will help slow the virus. We keep losing lives every day that passes. To quote Alex Orlando from Discover "It's caused the days to ooze together into a shapeless blob. Some struggle with loneliness, others might worry about their health and finances."

2020 was the year of the shortage of necessities. Toilet Paper, Alcohol Wipes, Hand Sanitizer just to name a few.

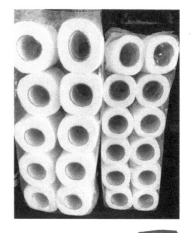

This are my personal reserves of Toilet Paper (don't buy online!) and Masks.

The Author

Janet Elizabeth Levy is a graduate of the Hard Knock University. She is an unknown amateur illustrator and this is her first ever attempt at publishing a book. This book with her personal illustrations are her reaction and a product of today's political atmosphere. She hopes you'll all enjoy them.

Janet is 76. She lives in a small rural town in Northern California, with her two dogs, and when in public, she always wears a mask!